PHOENIX RISING

PHOENIX RISING

SHARON M WALKER

Copyright © 2025 by Sharon Walker
All rights reserved. No part of this book may be reproduced in any manner whatsoever without written permission except in the case of brief quotations embodied in critical articles and reviews.
First Printing, 2025

Dedication

For my mother, Joyce.
One day we will meet again,
and together we will watch over all whom we love.
For now, I hope you are witnessing my rise and smiling

And

For all who wish to rise from the ashes,
your Phoenix awaits

A Letter To My Glorious Readers

Firstly, thank you from my core that you have entrusted me with your precious time here on earth to read my words. I am, and will always be, forever humbled by this act of kindness and connection.

With Phoenix Rising, my second collection, I wanted to offer words of inspiration that would illuminate the Phoenix within you. Her presence is enduring and if you allow her, she will soar high alongside you, especially in those moments where you feel you cannot rise once more.

Listen to her song, her quiet and gentle wisdom. She embodies the essence of growth, urging you to embrace the beauty in rising after every fall.

Trust in yourself. Trust you are loved. And more than anything, be brave in your conviction to live the life that is true for you.

I send you endless love and faith in your ability to rise, as your Phoenix holds you up from the smouldering ashes.

With love, S. Walker

Phoenix

The rise had been subtle
Like water simmering, quietly
Almost missable
She had hardly recognised the emergence
Once at boiling point, it had been too late
Her demise now a reality
She lay burnt and ragged in her slumber
Her slender arms wrapped around her face
Clutching tightly
Unable to witness what could be next
So tired from the fight within her
Resting
Breathing
She began to pull herself from her hiatus
A beautiful glow luring her to follow
As she tore herself from the earth
Dust clinging to her sweaty skin
She recognised herself once more
The phoenix inside propelling her upwards
Her wings would never allow her to fall again

Moat

The moat around her heart had been deep
No one could penetrate the dark depths
Or contemplate the tiresome swim
She made it easy for others to give up
Without guilt
Without care
With, daring the thought,
Relief
She never expected a different outcome
Almost relished in the knowing
Nothing changed
Safe in her heart
Alone no one could hurt her
Her sanctuary
And yet, her prison

Fierceness

It hurt
To be fierce
It hurt because she chose to change
Judgement followed
By others, yes
But more from herself
The glint of power subsiding
The second-guessing
The push to conform
Pressing her back down so she flattened
So she could be comfortable
Where everything made sense
And nonsense, dismissed
Like a queen with her maid
One hand flick, and she would be gone
Not unlike her fierceness
How swift she could be to discount her power
To sever ties with her true being
And yet
She understood the importance of her fierceness
Without it now, all she had conquered would be meaningless
A wasted breath
A wasted life
Compelled to exercise her stamina for growth

She took that important, expansive breath
As fierceness entered the room once more
This time, to stay

Leaf

The curled leaf huddled in the web
It's strong chains anchoring its home
Holding tight
The storm pushing through the valley
The wind never knowing, nor caring
What had been housed inside
The tiny spider
The heart of the leaf
Entrusted its safety unto it
Weathering the storm only half its burden
After the rain, the deluge
It would call on its braveness
Venturing outside
Rebuilding its broken, torn web
It's life
It knew with certainty
That if it could survive the violent storm today
Tomorrow would promise to be worth the last rain

You

When today ends
Quiet
Sounding only thoughts
Memories
Good, bad and yes, even ugly
Do you appreciate them all?
The light that intermittently shines into your window
The smell in your room from incense that extinguished hours before
The taste of red wine still stained on your lips
Closing your eyes
You listen intently and smile
Finally, after all the noise in your head subsides
There it is
Your beat
Your heart
Your lifeforce
I know you think everything else matters
But it doesn't
It truly doesn't
Only now matters

Just

Today I choose joy
Just being
Just my home
Just my furry friends
Just the simple pleasure of phone calls with my tribe
Just cooking soup and yummy treats
Just laughing at texts with friends
Just sipping red wine whilst writing
My favourite thing to do
Today I choose joy
And tomorrow I'll choose to do the same
Or something different
All I know is I'll still choose joy
That's what we were here to do

Source

As the ruby nectar from the vine cascaded down her throat
The warmth she felt came not from the wine, but from her heart
Together sharing a moment of serenity
As the light of the lamp glowed around her glass
Smudged fingerprints
A reminder of her uniqueness
The shadow played tricks on her eyes
She saw more than she wanted in that sweet space
She had thought only of despair and longing
It had faithfully visited when she beckoned
Unwillingly, peace replaced the torture
A pain she had begun to slowly enjoy over the years
It had been a devoted friend
Rising each moment when she yearned for validation
She had been a victim after all
Peace had no place here
And yet, she had no choice but to look
To feel
For this would be her true nature from now on
Weeping with the knowledge
What the source of her greatest joy should always be
Herself

Appreciation

Light smacked the leaves with such clarity
Illumination of such an ordinary green
Now magically transformed
Gloriously
Unable to turn her eyes away
Meditatively, the branches bounced in the soft breeze
As if allowing her to join in their daydream
Reaching into her
Reminding her
That darkness has its place
And light inevitably comes
Both are beautiful
Both are safe
Appreciation for the polarity
Revealed the hidden secret to life

Rainbow

I feel, in an unfeeling world
Where joy is found in the colour of a leaf
And a rainbow that magically appears
Seemingly from nowhere
I only needed to look up
How often had I not seen what had been in front of me
Behind the greyness of clouds, a rainbow patiently awaits
The sun breaking through the shroud
Showing itself in all its technicolour glory
That's how I now feel about life
My clouds come and go
Like gentle reminders that life needs them as much as the rainbows
Know my love
Your cloud will only stay for a short while
Eventually, the sun will claim its reservoir
Drying up the shroud in front of your very eyes
The rainbow of your life will come
So, feel in this unfeeling world
That's how you will find your rainbow

Sail

Readying to set sail
A new journey in her mind
At the very least, exciting
Her lesson of patience she had hoped, now learnt
Though she understood this lesson would be on repeat
A holiday from such growth welcomed
A reward for all she had accomplished
The hiatus, blissful
Serene
Standing at the bow
Allowing the wind to move past her
She could breathe in peace for a little while
Proud of the small awakening within
Knowing that awakening
Had been her greatest growth so far

Ground Hog Day

Do you ever feel like it's the same day
Over and over
On repeat
Where you spend your life learning
Trusting
And you finally get it
Only to die
Reincarnate
Possibly coming back to the very beginning once more
Only to relearn the lesson more painfully
My wish is to begin at my last ending
Where wisdom continues
Instead of relearning every lesson in order to heal
Exhaustion would never then to be an option

Karma

Does it really matter what they think of you
Whilst you sit on the chair
Your head in your hands
Expecting a different result
Believing in karma
One day you will wake from this moment
The hell that broke loose before, subsiding
Rewarding you for your efforts
Such a lie you have been told
There is no karma
There is only and ever will be
This moment
This time you have with yourself
Don't fall apart now
Not when you finally realise
The damage wasn't karma
It was brought on by yourself
Now is the time to rejoice
Freedom now a possibility
If you only allow it

Home

How funny is it
Where the days are long and tiresome
All that's great in those hours
Is the moment when you open the door
To the space that loves and welcomes you
Where the air in the room smells like you
And the feeling of soft clothes upon your skin
Cuddles
Nurtures
That's home

Myrtle Tree

As I look up through the myrtle tree
To see the mountain-ness gum
And the light of the day becomes iridescent
The colours so different in contrast within minutes
And I am alone with my thoughts
Circling within my head
Around my heart
Pushing and pulling
No direction
No clarity
Then the light bulb clicks me awake
Time to be brave now, she says
Do that thing you love
Before regret haunts you
Smiling, I thanked the trees,
The light
My Angels
And my soul

What if

What if you knew how many breaths you were given for your lifetime
What if you knew
You would change the way you view absolutely everything
Don't lie, you would
You would wake each day totally different to how you woke today
The unaware you
Without this constant remembering
Today you yawned yourself awake
And your mind began your day with how much sleep you didn't get
Not how much sleep you did
Then, without taking a breath
You think of all the things you must do today
You don't think, "Wow, the sky looks so blue through the window"
Or 'How happy the birds sound singing their morning song"
Don't wait for your next holiday to appreciate the sunrise
Don't wait for a special occasion to open the "good" bottle of wine
Don't you see
Every day you breathe is, in fact, the special occasion you yearn

Every time you are blessed to rise from your slumber
Or each moment your child looks at you with unconditional love
Or the laugh your friend has when she's telling a story
Don't wait to savour such absolute delights
True insanity is waiting for the grass to turn green on your side of the fence
It already is

Tribe

There's a difference between want and need
A needle-thin line
Differentiating a lust of ego
And a hunt for reunion with another
I say reunion because that's what it is
We've met before
In another life, another realm
Even when at first you don't realise it
You know the hunt is real
It's what makes you wake up each day
It should make you excited for each person you meet
Hoping they are one of those you have met
Before in past lives
Your tribe
The ones that have your back
Wanting them to witness your life, this new life
Your rise
Your growth
And you, of theirs

Leaving Behind

Trust is my friend
Faith, the unknown, my sister
Complacency has always been that narcissist in my life
The one who beckons me to stay as I am
Comfortable, safe, in total denial
Feeding my ego until it bursts with deception
Falling silent, I listen to the shadows in my heart
They cry out for the window to open
For the breeze to glide over my bare skin
Leaving behind the dark anger of the past
And a possible future
Breathing newness
Vibrant and alive
The past had been my gift
A learning greater than any teacher could offer
Leaving behind is never about saying goodbye
But saying, Thank you

Winning Hand

All I can think
Whilst the sea breeze rolls over my skin
Tingling every nerve into submission
And how the stars sparkle and glow
Setting alight both my eyes and my heart
The after-life better be amazing
Beyond belief
As I truly can't imagine anything better than this moment
Being
Being right now
In and of, this world
What a gift we have all received
The human experience
Don't waste this feeling
Not for one minute
We don't know if the grass is truly greener
After we leave
But don't hedge your bets
Know you have,
Right at this very minute,
The winning hand

Risk

The fly struggled on the screen
Trying to push through the barrier
Seeing the others on the other side, flying free
Pained to witness the terror of its prison
I noticed my empathy
The result of my own prison
Where jealously of something better, wearied me
Both of us forgetting freedom had its own kind of terror
They too, were at risk of pain
They just didn't know it

Moon Gaze

Bathing in moonlight
I felt it's healing power
Illuminating my skin
Glistening
I'm restless however
Trying to fix all the broken pieces
Of my outside world
Whilst my inner world, peaceful and serene
Left wondering why I am inviting in turmoil
That unwelcome guest who demands attention
The air stiff
The noise quiet
I cannot change the state of affairs
Only witness the flow with inevitability
The only way to dispel the agony
Willingly enticed upon my soul
Is to raise the white flag
And be gentle with myself
I close my eyes, awaiting the dawn
All I need do is love the lessons that present
And know that I am safely held under
The gaze of the moon

Scent

The combination of sandalwood and patchouli
Always calmed her
In ways she could never describe nor
understand, a memory of scent
Her greatest teacher at times when allowed the sensation
Like freshly mowed grass when just a little girl
A reminder of her father who slaved over the green fronds each week
She would sit in wonder of this great man
Looking forward to the day when she, too, would have one of her own
Both lawn and man
Neither, she realised now as a woman, necessary
She just wanted them
But the scent of sandalwood and patchouli stumped her
Now quieting her mind
Lives past, she remembered partly why she loved it
A feeling more so
Peaceful
Blissful
Joyful
Not the details
But the feeling was all she needed to move forward
That's how she wanted to feel always
And so, she did

Heart

I opened my heart a little wider
Allowing the light in
All that it is
And always shall be
Brilliant
Warm
Opening meant vulnerability
A chance of being hurt
Yet again
But what was the alternative
A life half-lived?
Even the feeling that past pain gave
Showing me I had been loved
At least for a little while
Hurt, still more wonderful than playing it safe
Loneliness so much more devastating
So, I'll open that heart of mine
Proud and wide
And trust the Universe has a new gift
Waiting just for me

Momentum

We were growing together
That magical time when we synced
Then something happened to me
Momentum fastened
Floundering spiritual growth
No longer an option
I asked you to hold on for the ride
To join me
But you couldn't keep up the pace
Sometimes I couldn't either
But I had no choice
It was exhilarating
Not knowing what was next to learn and feel
It scared you so you retreated
Within the dark corner, waiting
Thinking I may slow down
And come back to you
Trust me, I wanted to
It scared me too
How proud I am for my bravery
Knowing I would lose you if I reinvested in myself
Sometimes I shook my head in disbelief
You didn't know that, did you?
You could only despise what I was becoming
Losing that part of me that was you

But I eventually embraced the uncomfortable
Momentum gathering
Growth has many ugly parts
But it is the most beautiful gift
When the light hits
Breathing the freshest air ever breathed
That's how I know I'm on the right path
That's how I know growth was always necessary

Anthem

The soft breeze tickled the patient chimes
Gently playing its song of bells
Whilst crickets hiding in the garden,
Chanted their evening anthem
In the distance the ocean bellowed its roar
Accompanying the midnight band
Grateful for all who joined in
Even the bats' chatter enhanced this special ballad
I sat alone
Neither truly alone nor lonely
Secretly I loved it
Not desiring it to be a forever thing
But simply, for now
This moment
A slight but indulgent guilt blanketed over me
Whilst I wanted my love to hold me in his arms forever
I had known myself enough to be able to hold myself as well
For anyone who has been alone as long as I
Will know
Will understand
What I mean

Fireworks

We knew that night
Of the fireworks to come
Our life would explode into a million fragments
No chance of mending
The life we relied on, disintegrated
In front of our defeated eyes
What was your fear in that moment?
My terror overcame me
Knowing I couldn't love you anymore
Not like before at least
Were you the same?
Disbelief
Indifference
Disillusionment
All in that one tragic moment

Wings

It didn't take long these days to recognise the signs
Her weary eyes, blurred from past tears that had fallen
Far too many times to count
Echoing through her like a drop of water
Slowly spilling into a well
Resounding despair and clarity
All at once
This time must be different
Urging herself to find her wings
And in turn, her strength
So she could fly through the fire
Affirming she needed patience
Most of all, tenacity
Not just a "never say die" attitude
But more a "live now" one

Breath Held

The funny thing about clarity
It can become clear when it's all too late
Words said
Feelings hurt
Ties severed
The trick
The magic
Is catching it before such terrible deeds
The breath held
The most important moment before the next
The magic lies within those minuscule seconds
Before you speak
Cherish this space held
It has your best interests
That, I am certain

Heal

Awareness brings many feelings to the table
Ugly and cruel at times
Like "the band-aid effect"
Rip it off
Tend to your wounds
Raw and bleeding
But that air that touches your hurt
That's the healing
The awareness of all that has past
Is the healing
So let it

Because I can

Not because I don't love you
As I do
Or want to hold your hand
But alone time is precious to me
A time where I can check in
Have an internal chat about life
My feelings
My joys
My sorrows
Don't take it personally
I want romantic, sexy love
I want 'my person'
But please listen with intent when I voice this
I cannot be an extension of you
I am and should be, unique
As should you
I need those afternoons, sipping wine
Listening to music
Suffocating me by too much
Only turns my affections away
The woman you fell in love with is that woman
That independent, beautiful soul
Not the right arm of you
But whole
I sit now, present with myself

Sipping that wine
Listening to that music
Writing this
Why?
Because I can

Chase

For years
She chased all the wrong things
The wrong faces
The wrong places
The wrong occupations
Wasting her precious time on situations that couldn't fuel her
Safe had been her mantra
She lost her fierceness along the way
Until waking from her daze
Wondering why she would allow herself to be put in a box
A nicely ribboned one everyone liked her nestled in
Shiny and pretty
They were comfortable with her in there
She dared not risk their disapproval
And so, dimmed herself just enough for their acceptance
But no more
Something knocked her comfortable place
Pushing her out of that terrifying box
Naked and alone, she stood without guidance
She missed her trueness
Her rawness
Her fierceness
Safe stayed inside that box
She promised to never to reopen

Lullaby

Spoilt by chaos
Always surrounding her
Uptight had been the norm
Not concerning
But usual
So, when the oceans' hum entered her window
She smiled sarcastically
Knowing what its motivation to be
Almost betting it would lose the wager
But as she closed her unwilling eyes
To listen to its beauty
Its song
She relented and softly succumbed
Being right
Pure stupidity
If it meant missing out on the waters' lullaby

Wonder

I wonder why the light of the moon makes all things beautiful
Including me
Our romance to the moon
Like no other
Even the sun pales in its wake
It's glow regenerating us
And as I stood alone, looking up
The earth grounding me
I cried
As I felt it's love for me
I am never alone

Tinker

She tinkered with words
Like piano keys
Not knowing how they would sound
Forever embedded on the white bark
Ink spilled in her mind in technicolour
So many delicious words to select and arrange
Again, and again
Until she became the proud mother of the body of them
Their resting place, amongst the world

Eyes

Close your eyes
Don't concern yourself about what you can't see
Rather, more importantly, what you can
In that tiny world of darkness
That world is true
That world, if you let it, clarifies
All you worry about
All the wasted time
Really mean nothing
In the end
It means nothing
Trust in the light that comes after
It tells a song of hope
Of an unending smile
Of a tickle of a breeze touching your arm
And a spray of rain mist on your face
Clouds part so the moon can shine over your skin
How beautiful what eyes can see when open
But even more exquisite what they feel when closed

Breeze

As the breeze wafted gently through her window
She pondered, hoping it was a sign
A fresh start
Showering her skin with promises
Cleansing her battered heart
Even if it was just one
One new start
One new beginning
She would take anything
To stop this madness in her head
The constant aching of the past
A great deal to ask of such an element of the world
Instinctively, she understood her perception
The breeze hadn't been the answer
It had only been called upon by her soul
Merely to lift the veil
In order for her to move into her new world

Together

I see these lost souls
I walk amongst them
Feeling sympathy for their sorrow
Soon realising I play a part
I am them
Pity now feels awkward
Showing me an embarrassing reality
And a simple camaraderie
Together we can soothe our way out
From under the heavy rock
Weighing us down
Determined to keep us stuck
The abyss of unsettling fear
Together we can move mountains
And free ourselves
Together

Your truth

Truth
Your truth
Whether you say it
Whether you hide it
It comes out regardless
Truth
No matter how hard it can be
Is the only thing that brings peace
To you
To all who surround you

Ponder

Whilst I ponder why I am
Who I am
I question
What had it been that brought me to my knees
Shaking and afraid of who I could be
Would be
If I let it
Did my past hinder or help
Shedding light on lost love
And more love gained than I could possibly fathom
Such a fine line being loved so much
That some want to leave you in another's capable hands
And some want to rid you for their own relief
Both are love in different forms
Love for me
Love for themselves
It's how you choose to interrupt
And if you ponder long enough
Your answer will always be simple
Love

Girl

The feisty girl wants to say 'run and be free'
Hang the consequences
The scared girl wants to keep things familiar
Because at least, she knows its stable
The aware girl knows that both are right
And wrong, all at the same time
But she also knows that when the time is perfect,
That's when growth arrives at her feet
Begging her to notice
She will balance, becoming one with herself
That's when she births into a woman

Euphoria

How can I describe euphoria
When all the clicks sync
And the clogs in the wheel unite
Where the moonshine sings on water
And the raindrops smack the earth
Sending shivers where shivers rarely go
But go they must
Without consciousness of thought
The pure magic is that alone
That's euphoria

Renew

How volatile it can be
When you break free
From all you have been
Confusion setting in
Trampling every part of you
As you scramble helplessly
Demanding to make sense of the unsensible
But you do
Eventually, you need to
Growth cannot come without you
To renew
To let the past fall away
Like fragile rocks on a mountain side
And there you'll be
A now bigger and brighter version of you

Blackbird

On a warm summers' afternoon
The blackbird fled through the cornflour sky
It's speed chasing the last rays before nightfall
Knowing that every second mattered
In contrast to humans
Never quite understanding them
As most sped through life without thinking
Through childhood to adolescence
Through marriage and children
Only to arrive at a day where life confronted them
When regrets soothed them purposefully
Wishing nothing but acknowledgment of time wasted
Precious in its very essence
And yet, stupidly surreal in its lesson

Human

What is that feeling when a snail crawls past you
The sunshine piercing through its juicy body
Showing the intricate shell formation without it posing its beauty
Where the warmth in your heart for every living being
Separates you from others
Proving to you that you are not a monster
Loving the very essence the magic of life provides
Please see it, feel it
These tiny and minuscule moments make you what you yearn to be
Human

8759

The last hour of the year matters
It seems
Every smell
Every sound
Every taste
Matters
Why do we lay such pressure on one hour
In 8760 hours in one year,
We make one hour the most important
We profess we love someone
We say we will live better
Live truer
We promise to be better versions of ourselves
And when time clicks over to 1 again
We forget all the promises
Not so much to others
But the promises we make to ourselves
Please remember
No day, no hour is more special
Make that promise every day
To live, love and be
Every
Single
Day

Freely

I want to express freely
Without barriers
Without judgment
If I am withholding
Either for you
Or even, for me
I cannot be real
Eventually
I die slowly within
Not ever showing my trueness
The feeling of me
The essence
From my very source
Let me speak
Freely
So that clarity shall arrive
At the doorstep to our hearts

The Catcher

The ceiling fan methodically moved
The feathers of the dream catcher swaying
Like young lovers dancing
It had caught so many of her dreams in the past
Where in the early hours of the morning,
They were offered as a sacrifice
Releasing them
But her nightmares,
They were the ones it captured and held
Hijacking them in solitude
Holding them at bay
Awaiting the day she would dutifully address them
Where bravery would conquer her demons
But for the moment,
They sat amongst the softness of its feathers
Kindly and with grace,
Awaiting her

Soul

My soul connects with your soul
We don't need to be bound by blood
Secondary in my eyes
But the silver strands
The ones that bind us
Before we could speak
Before we breathed into this world
That's what matters
The shining, silver line anchoring
Resounding love into one another
Knowing that being alone will never be
Together our souls grow
And together we love this life ever more deeply
Finding each other
Loving each other
Being us

Decide

The greyness of the abyss had been alluring
Comfortable
Like the softness of a lumpy bed
I could be a victim there
Never needing to scrape my way out
Forever being lost
It made me special
The struggle made me illuminated to others
I liked that
Until I didn't
How did I find myself amongst these sad walls
Unable to pull myself up from the depths of insecurity
From diving too deep
Impossible to swim to the surface
It's a fine line
And a millisecond to decide
If lost is what I want
Or being found
What will save my heart
Decide

Ghosts

What is it when you are so happy
That you're sad
That all that has broken you
Now healed
And you are without a framework
The pain has gone
You are absent of the loss
Now needing to redefine yourself
That's when the sadness arrives
Where uncertainty creates its cruel melancholy
That's the sadness you are feeling
When you're so happy
And that's when it's time
To say goodbye to your ghosts

The Middle

I know, with all my heart,
That feeling you have right now
I've been there
More than once
Of being a little lost
Neither up nor down
Being in the middle is hardest of all
The trickiest to navigate
You're not euphoric
You're not sad
You're in the middle
Being lost in the unknowing
Of where to place your feet next
Offer breath into it
This is an important moment
Lean into its uncomfortable space
Be excited for the new version of you coming
It will be worth the angst
I promise you

Thaw

A freezer full of men
The ones that hurt me
The ones that I hurt
The ones that gave me hope
And the ones that let me down
Their names live in my freezer
Frozen in time
Until I decide to thaw them
Melting one by one
Saying thank you for their lessons
And more importantly,
Saying Goodbye

Crickets

The crickets chimed relentlessly
Never stopping for a breath
Until I listened
They wanted my awareness
And now that I am at attention
They fall silent
A cruel game
Alone in my thoughts
So I can dissect
Analyse
To stay awake till the early hours
Trying in vain to conquer my questions
To find the answers
They know I have them
I only need these quiet moments
Between their song and my breath

Stop

Is it fear that stops me
Every time I think I'm happy
Something else comes to threaten my smile
A forgotten bill
A silly argument
Concern for the future
Why don't I just trust
Everything always works out for me
The Universe has my back
The Angels stand loyally beside me
Holding my hand and my heart
And yet, I waste this precious time
On things that don't really matter
Not in the long run
I am certain that when I say goodbye to this beautiful world
My thoughts will be of love and laughter
When I gazed into my love's eyes
When the sea breeze danced along my cheeks
Not the worries or silly arguments
Nor the stresses life can bring
If I learn anything in this life
Let it be that I live for today
Today is all I have

Peace

Peace sometimes has its own type of torture
Where happiness knocks on your door too hard
Shocking your heart
Waking you from the ache that's been your life
It's a guilt of sorts
Knowing others feel no relief yet
Their turn hasn't come
But it will
It will
So don't succumb to martyrdom
Enjoy this peace
Whether long or short
It's your turn for joy
Take it

Purpose

There's a perfect time
When love enters your heart
Where all that hurt you, falls away
You did the work
The hard yards
Coming to a place where tears cleansed you clean
Where intimate moments with yourself held your hand
Knowing that if you could forgive yourself
For being lost
For being vulnerable
For being human
Would teach you the world
And your place in it
At that very moment, light pours in
Breaking the blackness that surrounds your heart
Oozing away the sludge of disappointment
Of sadness
Revealing the very purpose of your being
That is love
And that's all it should ever be

Grace

There are many times I think of you
You randomly pop into my head
Not just at times of sadness
Or of worry
But even when I'm so very happy
At peace
You come and visit my mind
I don't need you to anymore
I don't even want you to
But I do think of you sometimes
With love
And that's a good sign
A sign I have healed from you
I can finally leave with grace

One Time

There are a few times
In fact, more than a few
Where you remember what's special
What means something to you
Whether it be a phone call
Or a stranger's random smile
Or the wanted rain after a blistering summers' day
Maybe just as simple as opening your door
You're home
You're safe
Where the air never suffocates
But smells of you
Where time stands with you
Holding you
Knowing you must stop for a moment
Before you breathe deep once more
To begin again
A new day
With hope

Saviour

What defines us
When our tormented heart
Broken and burnt
Blackened ashes
Finishes smouldering
And begins to heal
Whether alone
Or within the shelter of a nurturing friend
It matters not
What matters is the realisation
The moment of clarity
Where your mind and heart become one again
That's when you heal
Where trust in vulnerability
Will be your ultimate saviour

Gone

While she listened to the loud echoes of the sea
The pounding waves reminding her how he liked her
A tiny fish floundering in his deep embrace
She tried to be small
To be silent
A timid mouse
Scared in the corner of her soul
Never allowed to be herself
She had long forgot that girl
The one that laughed too loud
And cried too hard
The one that displayed anger when she had been
Never releasing any emotions,
Except the love for him
That's why he stayed
He loved that small version of her
But like all truths, they eventually emerge
Sometimes without ever meaning to
She now presented him with her carefree, vibrant self
And then he was gone

Pink

The soft, pink clouds hovered around the moon
Like a blanket of marshmallow
Framing its brilliance
Smothered in its glow
I began to feel the depth of its energy
Pouring onto and into my cool skin
Penetrating deep within
Presenting me with divine beauty
I will never forget that moment
Messages from the heavens
We are never truly alone
I am never alone

Perfect

Sound rolled in
Gently at first
The thunder never really needing an invitation
Urging me to stop and listen
Mostly to stop
Then listen
To my voice
More roars
More depth of sound
Pounding
Why am I so scared of the thunders' voice
After all, it's only an angry cloud
Bursting to shake me free
A true friend only wishing the best
Only wanting me to listen
To me
To what I need to hear
That I am gloriously imperfect
And that, in itself
Is perfection

Message

I burnt the letter I wrote for you
My hand unsteady as I poured myself onto it
Spilling emotions
Forever staining the paper
Unsure if it had been me or other worlds
Urging me to extinguish it
Burning black, folding into itself
Cringing and crying
Heaving at the loss
Of what could have been
One tiny shred survived the ashes
One word remained
A message to take with me
To soothe my heart
'Love'

Stars

Not quite sure what had beckoned her to go outside
Leaving the comfort of her bed
But once the evenings' summer air nibbled her hot skin
She quickly succumbed, awaiting the reason
The crickets singing their song
Maybe hoping it would be enough
To stay with her thoughts
And this, she did
Being reminded of all things important
Like her breath
Her family
Her friends
The pure innocence of lizards playing in her garden
As if that wasn't enough
A bird fled past above her
Chasing to find its burrow in the trees for the night
That's when the magic of the stars came
Sending her a message
Reminding her they were tiny lights in the sky
Showing her the way to all that's beautiful
She forgot to smile
She forgot the simple beauty of looking up
At incredibility
At possibility
At hope

Fan

Rhythmically the ceiling moved
The fan obeying to its nature
Around and around
Responding to its ultimate use
Spreading air thinly within the room
Without prejudice
As she lay on the bed
Neither restful nor peaceful
She couldn't help but wonder
If the rhythm had been coaxing her towards serenity
In hope she would succumb to its very purpose
Had consistency been what she had ultimately wanted
Or an unnerving sense of what she didn't
Serenity hadn't been about her knowing her course
Maybe it had been about not knowing at all

Reflection

Upon reflection, I could feel him pull away
Or had it, in fact, been me
Sensing the change
No longer needing his adoration
Constantly validating
With grace, he took a bow
Retreating into the background
Where he would tenderly watch over me
And smile witnessing my rise

Sadness

There's something beautiful in sadness
It touches your heart gently
When every other part of you wants to destroy it
Wants to humiliate
Annihilate
But sadness cascades around you
Comforting you like an old friend
Until you are ready to cry yourself alive again
Never shout sadness away
Allow her to hold your hand
Until you're ready to let her go

World

There's another whole world inside me
Pulsing life in many forms
A glorious garden
Constantly budding new growth
In the past it has created blessed humans
Such an honour bestowed upon me
The world inside, not only blood and bones
But heart and soul
Where I war with my demons from past lives
Past bodies
Regularly forgetting why I fight them
This worlds' interior, a generous gift
It will love me till it's last breath
I will not take this for granted forever more

Stuck

My breath, stuck in a holding bay
Compounded by fear
With no place to go
Dying a little more with each second held
Looking for a chance to escape
Its nature had always been to survive
Whether I liked it or not
I had no choice
Not if I wanted to feel the kiss of the sun on my cheeks
Or the coolness the nights' darkness offers
Air finally exploding from my chest
Into the gloomy room
Left panting
Realising it had been time to live again

Lasting

I think we are all guilty of this
Of thinking we are not getting older
Of pretending we won't die
It only happens to others
We are empathic to the loss
Like Teflon on a saucepan
We skate off death in our minds easily
Quietly thinking ourselves an eternal human
Maybe that's what keeps us living
Our strive to breathe
Until one day, we are confronted with tiredness
We give up the fight
Finally
Knowing it was a good fight
And if, when we close our eyes for the last time
Certain we were loved
If we can do that,
We become eternal after all

Centre

Only I can tell you how I feel
Don't presume to know
You will be wrong
How could you know my heart
What it wants
What it needs
It isn't up to you
It has always been my responsibility
No one else's
All the conditioning of what love should be
Falling short of reality
Now felt, I know it to be so much more
A fullness like no other
And yet, I sit here alone
In complete knowledge of its existence
Even though I am the centre of it

Wind

The wind frightens me
Like no other element
The sun can burn my lost intentions into oblivion
Scorching them forever from my mind
Rain can wash away my past
The sky crying for my wrongs
Cleansing me of past sins
The earth beneath my feet, soft
Letting me sink into her warmth
Like a mother cradling her child to soothe
I should not despise the wind
More so, to honour it
It blows away cobwebs of past mistakes
Lifting up the veil
Revealing the causes of them
Leaving me bare so I can start anew
Maybe I'm afraid of the wind
Because that would mean a bravery I'm yet to master

Freedom

Feel what you feel
Whether great joy or great loss
Feel it
Own it
Express everything
Hold back nothing
Feel in an unfeeling world
Where we are taught to hold back
Not to show ourselves
Raw and without guilt
We hide our true nature so often
Thinking people will love the façade
The version society deems acceptable
Don't dilute anything about you
As one day, so watered down
You'll float silently away
Trust these words
You will be loved
By the right people
You never need to pretend again
That's what true freedom feels like

Birthday

Two hours to go
Before the clock ticks over
Another year
Another journey
So fast and yet,
Lessons took forever to reveal
Eternally grateful for all of them
That's what birthdays do
They remind us of the year that passed
Of promises made
Kept or not
To be better
Happier
More kind and thoughtful
Like New Years' resolutions
But these promises, quietly stronger
Secrets unto themselves
No other really knows that birthday wish you make
Before the second hand clicks to a new year
But you do
And that's all that matters

Our Dance

I love dancing with her
When I quiet my chatter in my mind
And I feel her deep within my heart
Where she resides for me eternally
I take her for granted most days
That internal friend who forgives my short comings
My forgetfulness of her
Sometimes though, there's a song we dance together
Entwined, we swirl around like elegant ballerinas
Gloriously lifting our arms
Free, away from all others
Just us
Heart and mind, entangled
The perfect balance

Trust

She understood the detriment of her thoughts
And yet, found it impossible to stop them
Particularly in the early hours
Where time drudgingly dragged its feet
Each moment thinking of the terrifying future
Harming her beyond her current world
Stopping would be like saying goodbye to an old friend forever
The one who intimately knew her doubts
Her limited expectations
But who also knew that if left to her own devices
She would fly in another direction
One that would have her rise beyond even her own belief
How exciting that world would be
If she could only trust herself

Listen

I want to listen to you
Your advice
Your wisdom
What I need to heal
I want to listen to you
It's easy when it's dark and quiet
But it's when hell is breaking lose
Where delirium overtakes
That's the important moment
When you hold my hand
You tell me all the time
"You've got this"
That's what I love about you
You're my cheerleader
No one will ever understand me like you do
So I will listen
And remember you are my greatest strength
You are me
And I, you

Shell

As she strolled along the shoreline
Scouting seashells
The awaiting ocean, patient
As she gently tossed the unbroken ones back
Hoping or at the very least, wondering
If inside still contained a little urchin
In need of help from its overnight beaching
To be given a lifeline for another chance
In the mighty body of water
She wanted to save them all
Knowing that would be an impossible task
At times, she had felt exactly like troubled urchins
And by some miracle, an Angel in disguise had appeared
Throwing her back
Taking care not to smash her precious shell against the rocks
When heartache came to visit
As it is guaranteed to do in this world at times
Paying it forward gave her a sense of gratitude
For her past saviours and now for herself

Balance

Water finds its own level
In my glass
In my bath
As I playfully rock it from side to side
Enticing it to settle
To balance
Like the ocean
Loving the waves of disruption
Echoing shadows and light
Up and down
Good and bad
When the wind stops
The ocean falls silent for a moment
Balancing
Regaining its strength
So it can start all over again

Insecurity

Insecurity seeped in
Prowling around her body
Pawing at her thoughts
Niggling tiny scenarios into her mind
Like they were already realised
She understood what was happening
But felt powerless to stop them
Finally, for a moment, she halted them
As soon as she relaxed
Feeling superior
They devilishly smiled
Readying for another bout of 'what ifs'
To play in her mind
Her task now was not to fight them
The only way to win the demons' game
Who fervently entered her mind
Had been to let them pass
Like a stranger in the street

Kryptonite

The wind outside screamed at her door
It's winter ice endeavouring to crack at its seams
She chose to look away
Instead, hypnotically staring at the shadow on the wall
Of the branches outside that cunningly entered her room
Playing a game in her mind
Within her walls
Drawn to the swaying shadows
If she stayed too long in this state, whilst serene
It could be her kryptonite
Never wanting to leave this quiet, sacred space
Never risking failure
Potentially destroying her
She needed to balance the beauty within
And the harshness outside her
If she stayed, she risked never falling
But falling had been where her greatest strength appeared
So why stop now?

Version

A single tear paved its way down my cheek
As I listened intently to my inner voice
Marking the hopeful clarity I longed for
Almost begging its arrival
The tear represented my relief
The words, softly spoken
The images that came alive, exciting
Witnessing a possible new version of myself
Lighting up in my mind's eye
I like her, this new version
So confident and humble in her gift
Unashamedly trusting this is where she's meant to be
Now the old version, whilst lovely
Must exit gracefully
So I can welcome the new version
She will serve me well
In the years to come

The In-Between

You know the feeling of being lost
When happy gives no direction
No Strive
And sad, leaves you spent
Soberly
We should want happy, right?
To want nothing more
As sad is so exhausting
Who wants to be the un-dead
Tell me what's the in-between
How do you name it
Whatever you call it,
That's the sweet spot
That's when you feel the most alive
I call it peace
Where the two collide
And all you need to do is live

Uncomfortable

It's not that awful
Being uncomfortable at times
Squeezing out of that zone
The comfort zone
Uneasy teaches
If you're willing to open up
Be vulnerable
Greatness is within you
Moments come and go
Never staying long
Resilience is your nature
Fighting for you in the background
When times are tough or uncomfortable
Believe in your abilities
Listen to its lesson
You won't regret it

Within

What you see on the outside is beautiful
However, there is a world within me
Where beauty isn't defined
It just is

Success

No longer do I measure my success by money
Like a well-played monopoly board
How many, if any, houses I've accumulated
Whilst I love that feeling
After all, I am human to an extent
I love more how I feel now
When I close my eyes at night
After a day with a friend or my child or my love
Where our laughter or shared thoughts matter more
Where an embrace or hand held warms me up so much
My heart swells
Where my sigh of satisfaction breathes life into me
Caressing my heart to stay beating
At the end of the day
A satisfied sigh reveals
Love surrounding me
That is success

Colour Of Love

If love were a colour
What would it be?
An auburn sunset
Touched by a tangerine hue
Passionate and vibrant
The colour of hope
Or maybe the colour of the sea
Shades of light and dark blue
Showing the depths we go
To award ourselves belonging to another
Or maybe it's an earthy green
Grounded in the knowledge that you love
And are loved
Perhaps yellow, the colour of joy
Where laughter fills you up so much you burst
I believe
Love is a rainbow
The perfect balance
That's how I want to love
That's how I want to be loved

Acknowledgements

To my daughters, Taylor and Madeleine who never falter in their encouragement and belief in me and in my words, I thank you.

To Taylor, my marketing guru, for all your hard work in helping with the final read through, my gorgeous website and Instagram page.

I love you both beyond worlds. You are the biggest loves of my life.

To my mother, Joyce (who has now sadly passed). You have been the one who taught me to rise, even when I wanted to cower. You have been the one to show me unconditional love for others and for myself. I strive every day to be the best mum I can be to our girls and I know without a doubt, that you are smiling as you witness my rise.

To my tribe, my beautiful friends that constantly amaze me with your love and support.

To Steve, who gently entered my life and my heart.

I would also like to thank the precious ones who believed in Serenity's Path, my very first collection. To Triarna (A to Zen), Hiam (Totally Active Healing) and Lauren (Coming Home Healing) for housing and in turn, selling numerous copies in their stores. What a surreal feeling to see it proudly sitting on your shelves.

To the talented Betsy Marks, who has yet again, created the most beautiful and perfect art to don my cover. My Phoenix is stunning. She will be forever eternal and I, forever grateful of your gift.

To Leanne & Gab, who understand my shyness towards all things technical. I adore my book cover. You are both so very special to me.

And finally, to the ones who read my words and gave me such wonderful feedback that my words have helped and connected with them. Your belief in me, propelled and encouraged me so much that Phoenix Rising was born. I now cannot stop creating and know with such certainty, this is my true path, so I thank you from the depths of my heart.

www.ingramcontent.com/pod-product-compliance
Lightning Source LLC
Chambersburg PA
CBHW052141070526
44585CB00017B/1925